PUBLISHED by PARABLES
Earthly Stories with a Heavenly Meaning

Helpful Holy Hints – Drifting Through Daffodils, The Dream Fields of Destiny
By
Judy Martin Davis

Helpful Holy Hints- Drifting through Daffodils, The Dream Fields of Destiny
By Judy Martin Davis

Published By Parables
June, 2021

All Rights Reserved. No part of this book may be reproduced or utilized in any form or by any means, electronic or mechanical, including photocopying, **recording, or by any information storage and retrieval system, without permission in writing from the author.**

      Printed in the United States of America

Readers should be aware that Internet Web sites offered as citations and/or sources for further information may have been changed or disappeared between the time this was written and the time it is read.

Helpful Holy Hints – Drifting Through Daffodils, The Dream Fields of Destiny
By
Judy Martin Davis

Helpful Holy Hints

PREFACE

The Mighty Move of God is in motion with these Helpful Holy Hints. They will help motivate, inspire, and empower your journey called life. They create that extra spiritual push needed to get through the many challenges that the enemy has bombarded upon the lives of the Saints. Seek the only means of spiritual security and solitude you need to make a difference in your quest for excellence by standing strong, steadfast, and unmovable during these times of uncertainty. I am excited and full of gratitude as I first give all the Glory to God from whom all blessings flow. I dedicate this first special project to my mother, the late, great Jessie Thomas Martin. To my family, my Spiritual Team, that is too many to name individually, Kathleen Harrison, Claudette Range, Jessi Mapes and The Mapes Mob, Minister Sheila Madison, Pastor Carnell Bailey, and Alexander Adams, Latesha Rogers Dorsey, and Pastor John Jefferies. Last but certainly not least, to all the Saints of God who have used the Power of Prayer, fasting, Wisdom, and the Word of God to Speak Life into the atmosphere and my Spirit to make this dream a reality. So, where do we go from here to eternity?

"Keep it Moving Forward in Jesus Name".

The beginning of Great Destiny is in the daffodils

She showed up out of nowhere, abandoned in a devastated mess combined with divorce, very little money, and a whole lot of internal pain and anguish. But the dream fields that resided in her soul were the outlets that released the misery of all those harbored feelings of hurt and gloom. They are the masters, the dream fields! My mother attended First Emmanuel Missionary Baptist Church, pastored by the late George Rogers Clark. Pastor Clark was very anointed, when he preached, you felt the presence of God. I was baptized at age 5 during a spirit-filled revival. Pastor Clark asked, how many people love the Lord and not ashamed to let anyone know? I felt the burning of the Holy Spirit moving in my soul, and before I knew it, I had made my way to the altar and was baptized the same night. I remember after such a massive submerging in this large baptismal pool. Then I was soon seated on the front seat on the right side of the church, fell asleep and the pastor threw has handkerchief and woke me up. I remember shouting NO! The whole church laughed, and I was spanked by my mother for not being attentive. Saints would always ask if you were yet holding on, especially in the COGIC Holiness Church, pastored by the late Elder General Watts. This church was on fire for the Lord, and each Sunday I would sneak out and run as fast as I could across the lot to the COGIC church with the upbeat soul-stirring music. Pastor Watts was a powerhouse of prayer and the people were peeling off the misery and stress of life's many challenges. There were many signs and wonders of the movement of God. These wonders allowed the Saints to channel and send feelings good or bad to their proper atmosphere a place of refuge and strength. My mother was a hardworking LPN nurse who worked at the Baton Rouge General hospital for 27 years. We were rock-bottom broke, lived on, Howard, Alice, and Letts worth Streets just to name a few. I remember moments of many difficult times that really stuck out in the daffodils of my memory. I was only 10, we rented a house from Mrs. Charlotte Reed. One day she came over to collect the rent and informed us that her daughter was moving to Louisiana and needed a place to stay, and we needed to move within 30 days. This news devastated my mom. I remember when Ms. Reed left; my mom went into a soul cry to the Lord for a house to rent. God answered. The neighbors hated to see us go, but they used the resources they had to find a house not too far away. They used their trucks and cars and helped move to the house on Lettsworth Street owned by Mr. Theotis White. Mr. White was a tall, large man who wanted rent paid early and had no problem asking. He increased the rent, the house was leaking and had floor issues just to name a few. Once again God heard the soul-cry of this Christian woman whose purpose in life was to take the little she had and make someone else's day. She lived like a pauper to give like a princess. She worked long hours ironing as a side job along with sitter's jobs to supplement our income. We soon moved to Alice Street and was very blessed to meet wonderful people who took up the fight of poverty by sharing whatever they had to bridge the gap. They made sure everyone around was able to eat and enjoy some of the small yet fundamental things in life. The atmosphere made everyone so unified and willing to help. Greater Mount Gideon, Baptist Church, the church that was only 3 houses down, would always put young people to work for the Lord. The church mother who lived next door heard me singing one day and she recommended me for the church choir. I remember the first time I went there one Tuesday evening, prayer and testimony service was going on. People would sing a powerful hymn, then prayer and testimony would follow. I was standing in the small circle of maybe 12 people, and then finally it was my turn the old church mother Mattie White belted out a song and by the time she was done singing, I ran out of the church fast as I could in fear of praying out loud. I made it home and my mother was wondering why I was almost out of breath. I told her I was chased by a dog and that he almost bit me. Liar, liar pants on fire. She laughed and soon after there was a knock at the door. Oh no, standing there were Pastor Howard and his wife. They explained what happened and the belt met my behind and then the apology soon followed. The next step was restitution by appearing next Tuesday, singing a song, and saying The Lord's Prayer along with another apology for those present. That was another daffodil in my walk to this destiny. At age 11, I started working as a dishwasher at LSU Pentagon Hall. While working there, I met a young man whose name was Lester Brown. Lester was a graduating senior at McKinley High School. He was working to pay for his graduation supplies. Lester was a tall slim guy with such kind demeanor, very helpful, he was my pretend older brother. He was very thin, but very strong. As life flowed on through the helpful holy hints of these dream-fields, I am reminded how many times at home were often difficult, not enough food, money, clothes were handed down from one of mom's employer's whose build was on the style of an adolescent age 13. Mrs. Louise Sutton, what a doll. She died April 2, 1980 and left a $5,000 settlement for my mom. Many challenges presented themselves to stop that money from being in possession of my mom, but with lots of fasting and prayer, God answered. My roots and spiritual youth training came from Greater Mount Gideon Baptist Church. As a youth I have sung in the children's and young adult choirs. I worked in the Baptist Training Union and Home Mission Ministries along with weekly prayer meeting and testimony services. After years of training and great teaching I was given my ordination and ministerial licenses. I was working faithfully in 3 churches. First Emmanuel who had early 7:00 a.m. services which allowed me to go to Sunday school at 9:30 and by 10:15 I would wrap up to make it to Mount Gideon in time for 11:00 a.m. services singing the young adult church choir. I was active in the (BTU) Baptist Training Union along with the Home Mission and alternated with Elder General Watts in the Church of God in Christ which was very active and upbeat to say the least. Each Wednesday evening around 7:00 p.m. prayer meeting was implemented in many houses in our neighborhood. Evangelist Lillian

Helpful Holy Hints

Bradford and my mother was promoting this wonderful movement and most of the neighborhood was on board. Oh, how they would sing, pray, and testify about the goodness of God. This is the reason I am so locked into the faith; my prayer life got stronger in the things of God and allowed many great chances to grow and work in the community and go to school at the same time. What a blessing. I got my next summer job as a receptionist at the McKinley Middle School, which was the kick-start to launching my training as a receptionist. I still worked at Pentagon Hall part-time in the evening and was promoted from a dishwasher to checking student ID's. /cashier. I answered phones in the McKinley Middle school office under the supervision of Mrs. Marion Lastrapes. Mrs. Lastrapes was a stickler for perfection, so proper, proud, prim, and perfect. Soon the summer was over but after school, I got a great opportunity to work with Mrs. Eula Mae Hatter, (aka) Cuzzin Carrie along with Mrs. Mary Mason Gordon of 1460 WXOK. These ladies were both unique in their own way and served as the launching pad to learn the ropes of radio. In those days, there were reel to reels, 8-track tapes along with 45, 33 and 78 records. It just did not get any better. Children back in those days respected their elders, ate their vegetables, and said their prayers remembering

who ruled the roost, adults ruled, children drooled. During my time at the studio, I met some interesting people, Bob Stewart aka Solomon Kincaid who worked the graveyard shift was one of my favorites. During those days in production Bob showed me many ways to let the music work for you. I soon met the late great Guy Brody in the 80's when Rapp now Hip-Hop was the newest kid on the block in music. I went to work at "The Beat" radio station that was a short career, I was training on air with Guy Brody at the age of 17. Guy was promoting a Michael Jackson concert and worked himself into a mad frenzy over the lack of community not buying tickets, the police were called. The station closed. I left the station and back to square one job hunting for work in the radio industry-full-time. But somehow God had a ram in the bush and that ram in the job search market was the department store D.H. Holmes. I worked as a salesperson in the bed/bath and linen department, under the management of Mrs. Ruth Junker. The team consisted of 6 amazing ladies and one gentleman who really worked hard to keep us motivated while moving in the right direction.
I learned to cook my first pot of red beans on the cooking show of the late Vernon Roger of channel 9, that we featured out of our store each Wednesday in the housewares department. Let us

talk social. God knows that we are social creatures, not always going where we need to go, however, I was out one night with some friends and met a man whose name was Edward Kwiatkowski, a very tall handsome German man with a very beautiful and captivating smile. STOP! Hold that thought and take a dose of these helpful holy hints. Don't you stop reading, because after your dose of Helpful Holy hints keep reading!

These are some Helpful Holy Hints to empower the inner you and reflect and focus on the Goodness of God in these last and evil days.

Judy Martin Davis

God Prevails!

HELPFUL HOLY HINTS

Monday- Remodel your mindset and become a remarkable role-model for the Almighty- Monday!

Tuesday- It is a Must to take the Rust out of your trust-Tuesday.

Wednesday-Weight loss at sensible cost makes you healthy, wealthy, and wise, Wednesday.

Thursday- Take the Victory trolley to triumph over trials and tribulations- Thursday.

Friday- Farewell to the fireworks of fear and frustration-Friday.

Saturday-Saints sifting Satan as wheat as we make a solid spiritual foundation and say so long to sorrow- Saturday.

Sunday-Make a solid your spiritual foundation and say so long to sadness Sunday.

Judy Martin Davis

More Helpful Holy Hints

Monday-In the midst of the madness, miracles are making their way to a Mighty Manifestation-Monday.

Tuesday-Tear off the turbulence of Spiritual turmoil- and Target the beauty of breakthrough and burst through the bounty of your brokenness with boldness-Tuesday. Tuesday.

Wednesday-Don't' waddle in weakness; rise up in wellness-Wednesday.

Thursday-Tackle tough times of torment and bad temperament with a ticket of Godly opportunities of thankfulness-Thursday.

Friday-The final phase of favor is the fruitfulness of fruition.-Friday.

Saturday- Seeking the Savior is the satisfying solution to sanctification and soul salvation-Saturday.

Sunday-Set the standard in Saintly servitude that will satisfy the Savior Sunday.

He walked over to the table after staring for a while, introduced himself and suddenly asked me to dance. We danced; we talked and then exchanged telephone numbers. Soon after we started to see one another for long periods of time and then out of the blue we fell in love, and he asked me to marry him. I was so excited that he wanted to build a life together, then the dark side of the daffodils surfaced, one month before the wedding, he was killed in a motorcycle accident, and I was left to pick up the pieces. Then after a year of grieving I met a man who once again swept me off my feet. Finally, I was beginning to see the light of day. He proposed we had a fabulous wedding then I became pregnant and the death of our first child put a wall that diminished our marriage. It was a sad day, we became distant, and then we became pregnant again, this time we were headed to divorce court. We welcomed our son, Stuart Paul Wilkerson. He was born 7lbs 8oz. cute as a button; however, the joy of his arrival just could not mend that hurting marriage that was too far gone. I then went to work at Thrifty car rental as an agent. I soon met this tall handsome man, who was and still is tall, handsome, and so slim, long narrow feet, great teeth, and bedroom eyes. He was honest and forthright. He told me that he was ready to settle down and I really wanted a chance to find myself and really make marriage work this time. James Ray Davis won my heart and the heart of my mom, he was such a great friend, and however, I was in love with him and in denial at the same time. We were soon married and welcomed our son James Reginald Davis.

I decided to go back to work full time since my mom wanted to keep the boys and spend time with them, I was blessed with a job at Ethyl Corporation. I started as a temporary mail clerk, doing radio on an as needed basis. I met a woman, Sue Marston at Ethyl who recommended me for her job as the switchboard operator, she retired and there I was set to work at Ethyl. The gloom and doom loomed and made its way to my home when my son Stuart was diagnosed with Neuroblastoma Cancer, a cancer that was destroying his nervous system. Because of his age, the younger patients 6 months and younger are the better candidates for the limited treatment which gave better chances for survival. We went to Dr. Danny Wood for a fall, Stuart collapsed one day while playing at school and was unable to get up. Dr. Wood is a brilliant doctor with a heart of gold. He immediately agreed to see us and admitted Stuart into Our Lady of the Lake Hospital and performed a series of tests then determined Stuart had Neuroblastoma Cancer. We were then referred to oncologist Dr. Shelia Moore of Earl. K. Long. hospital. Dr. Moore is someone who would remind you of that firm but fair grandmother. She has so much heart for her patients, just as Dr. Wood. He is still very kind, caring and soft spoken. What a guy! The journey soon began to change drastically from a working mother to a mother of a child with cancer. I had to quit my job June 15, 1989 and the journey with Stuart and cancer treatment immediately began. Stuart and I moved to Memphis, TN and off to St. Jude's hospital we went. We were given oncologist Dr. Laura Bowman, she was amazing. She gave so much information and great care to all our concerns. We lived in Memphis coming back and forth to Baton Rouge, from June 16th, 1989 until January 1991. We flew Northwest Airlines now closed, often stayed at the Riverfront Hotel on Beal Street; we targeted the Rondeveau barbeque restaurant every chance we got. Stuart went into remission and soon relapsed. The dark daffodils of death struck my family with sending Stuart home to die which he did, February 1, 1991 at his grandmother's house where he wanted to be. I was devastated watching him lose his beautiful face and strength to become totally helpless. He was my first child that lived, the daffodils of destruction and death encamped

Helpful Holy Hints

around my family and then suddenly all hell breaks loose again. The diagnosis of Leukemia for my mom and a severe heart condition for my aunt and godmother, Gertrude Thomas Walton. Both sisters were totally different, but unique. Gertrude was the oldest, a woman of grace, cocky yet confident and very generous to me. She took excellent care of me especially as a baby. She wanted my parents to let her, and Uncle Bob adopt me, and she was willing to pay, however my parents refused and that kept her at bay for settling for just being my aunt and godmother. Uncle Bob Walton, her husband was a humble man, often mistreated by his wife. He gave her everything she wanted, but it was never enough. He worked off-shore as a deckhand at first for Chotin Barge-lines for 40 years. At retirement, was injured, he sued the company won the lawsuit and was re-hired as head chef for the company. I remember when he received his 30-year service watch just before the injury he was elated. Even though he was unable to read, write or spell, somehow, he managed to talk about world affairs as if he was a college graduate. He was multi-talented with many gifts, he was a master builder, built and painted his house from the ground up. He served as head-deacon of the Beulah Baptist Church for over 50 years until his health failed. He mentored many youths, expounding on letting them know that the wage of sin is death, but the gift of God is eternal life through Christ Jesus. He blessed all he met, with his award-winning smile, his home-made doughnuts that would put Krispy Kreme to shame, and the gift of teaching and sharing his knowledge of the bible. I remember him always saying these words of wisdom; The Bible is right, and somebody is wrong, but not the bible. He loved his family, even though there were no children born to this union, I was as close to having a child that they would ever have. My uncle Bob died; however, I remember many great things about him, and how he implemented holiness and good Godly wisdom. That is what he instilled in me for life. He was a one heck of a checker player, beating him at a game of checkers was unheard of. The years passed and one early morning I received a phone call from my cousin Doris Hardnett informing that she had stopped by to say hello to my aunt Gertrude. She rang the doorbell, no one responded. Doris suggested we check in on her. My mother and I went to check things out and there were 13 locks on the door. We called the police, they broke the door, and my mom found my aunt lying in bed deceased dressed in her Sunday best suit, hat, shoes, and stockings. She also had all policies along with her last will and testament. I was

Helpful Holy Hints

seated on the porch just blown away of her passing. It was a very dark day once again for our family. Once again we were all heartbroken again. We were devastated but could not display the pain as aunt Gertrude hated her sister and wished her dead just as she wished my uncle Bob. The darkness of the daffodils was very strong and stirring the atmosphere of hurt, shame and confusion. But God! When my aunt Gertrude died in 1995, my god-sister received her portion of the estate and as for the rest, my mother was able to stop working and do very well financially which was much deserved. Since she was left out of the will, I was able to give mom my aunt's car buy her little house she was renting for 200.00 monthly for 10,000. Mrs. Lillian Baines, mom's amazing land lady was addicted to my seafood gumbo since my mom had cancer, Mrs. Baines felt that giving my mom free rent was her way of being a blessing. Mom soon went into remission for a little while and then relapsed July 1996. There were now more doctor appointments, blood work and the whole 9 yards as it was for my son Stuart and my aunt Gertrude. My mother passed away August 31/Sept 1996 @ midnight, at the new Baton Rouge General Blue-bonnet location. Only 1 word, DEVASTATED! Reggie was 8 years old, and my husband was working I called him and as he rushed to the hospital, he was numb, nearly lifeless. I stepped in the hall to alert Christy her nurse of mom's passing. I had nothing left to cry, no tears would come, my heart was racing, and the tears were still not flowing. She left me, and I felt like an abandoned puppy in the snow with nowhere to go. I thank God for the talk she had with my best friend the late Sheila Hilton, who loved me dearly as a mom/sister friend. She shared with Sheila that now that I am dying mom said softly, please look after Judy. Sheila was the glue that kept everyone together; she was mother-sister and very best friend. She was gold with so much beauty and heart. She owned Hilton and Company dress shop, she was Hilton, and I was company. We had over 30 years of sister-ship. Her birthday was literally celebrated 3 times. JR's birthday is July 1, Sheila's birthday was July 2 and Jay Reginald's birthday is July 16. We called it the trio birthday. 3 people who had 3 parties. I remember when my son Reggie was 16 years old, and I asked her what did she want for her birthday? She replied with no hesitation, the honor of christening Reggie was her response. Request granted. After Sunday services the following Sunday at Greater King David Baptist Church, Dr. John E. Montgomery III. performed the christening in his office and we went out to eat afterwards, we had a blast. Shelia has gone on to be with the Lord, after secretly

Helpful Holy Hints

battling cancer my worst enemy. However, she has left a life-changing lesson how important it is to not only tell someone you love them but show them. She was the sister I never had, and she always made us feel inclusive in every holiday, every celebration just no matter what, she treated me like a sister a mother and a friend all rolled into one. My son Reggie graduated Glen Oaks High School with honors making Most Outstanding Boy from freshman to senior year. He went on to Nichols State University of Houma, LA. He did not have a car yet and his dad and I were car hunting. We found a pearl white, 2004 Mitsubishi Galant and my co-worker; Georgia Harris and I drove the car to Houma to pick up Reggie. He was standing outside looking for us and we were looking at him. I called and told him to come to the ivory car to his right, he was so tickled as he drove us back to Baton Rouge. Georgia jokingly shouted out my God boy can you drive any faster, it is getting dark out here. We all laughed. Having him home for the weekend was such a treat. Many great Sunday meals and care packages sent back with him as he traveled back and forth. Soon he transferred to ULL in Lafayette, Louisiana where he graduated with honors in Political Science with a concentration in public administration. I dreamed that he would go to Southern University but his career, his choice. I can say that he paid for his own college education, the only thing we gave were monies for food and other miscellaneous allowances. Reggie is all grown up, working at the State Capitol and teaching at his old High School Glenoaks High Panthers. We are so proud. I still want that degree from Southern University Law Center, that is my sincere prayer. FIX IT JESUS! I keep trusting God and staying humble and grateful for each day that he keeps my family circle strong and alive. I thank God for my committed life to community service and here and abroad. I live each day as if it is my last to serve people as Christ did. I get up reminding myself that if I am in God's Lamb's Book of life, ALL IS WELL. When I leave this world, I am referring to this ready writer scripture where it says in Mathew 25:23 His Lord said unto him, Well done, good and Faithful Servant; thou hast been faithful over a few things, I will make thee ruler over many things: Enter thou into the joy of the Lord. I state these scriptures to emulate the truth of the bible how it relates to everyday living, and when these principles are applied daily to the problems, challenges, and vicissitudes of this life you will get great success in all that you encounter. GOD IS SO GOOD! When Reggie graduated and moved out to at least 4 states to start, Newport News, Virginia, Smithfield, North

Carolina, Miami Florida and finally Washington D.C working for the campaign to Elect Barack Obama for President time 1. I thank God for all the opportunities that gave my son the political background to work the campaign a second time and make the Obama alumni organization. The daffodils of life have blessed me with so many wonderful gifts of opportunity that will last a lifetime. I am encouraged and empowered inspired and motivated yet humbled to be a part of the unshakeable Mighty Move of God. In-spite of all the illnesses and my family circle being broken I am still here, alive, and well. Thank you, Jesus, for my journey called life. Okay let us talk work! I went to work at channel 33 with some amazing people. Cyril Vetter was the owner and we got along like family. I enjoyed the journey of TV and radio for almost 10 years. I remembered when I applied for the job it was for a job in traffic. However, I felt because of my radio on air experience that I needed to start somewhere, and this would be another learning experience for me. Somehow, I ended up taking the receptionist job there instead. I replaced a lady whose voice just did not cut the mustard and I worked in various areas of the organization, from making commercials and assisting with the Jerry's Kid's Telethon, to traffic and sales. I ended up being asked to work in traffic as the traffic manager on a temporary basis while Doris Perkins was having surgery. I worked in traffic for 8 weeks after a very intense 2-week training. There are times in my life when I reflect on how God has allowed me to encounter so many great people in my life, like Doris Perkins just sweet, is what she was. Now to knock this Favor up a notch. I recall in 2003 when I started being very active with Southern University, as a young woman I was always fascinated with the band the football team and the entire on the bluff atmosphere. I went to Birmingham, Alabama where Southern University played and won the 2003 SWAC Championship. I was an avid fan of Mama Jag and not to mention our 2003 quarterback, Quincy Richard. He reminded me of another one of my favorite quarterbacks Terrance Levy who played from 1998-2001 and was so excited about football, Levy later passed on and that was a dark day of tragedy, but my love for him as his honorary mom will always remain. My favorite person on that campus was the wonderful late Jewel Jefferson Durr, affectionately known as "Mama Jaguar-Southern University Baton Rouge. We met in 2003. I took the 3:00p.m. flight back to Baton Rouge and met Crystal Hill who was the cook for Mama Jaguar. When I met Crystal, she was so kind and when she invited me over to meet Mama Jaguar, I was so excited I purchased the SWAC

Helpful Holy Hints

Championship T-shirt, hat, and shakers. When I entered the door that was always opened, I saw the most loving and kind woman I had ever met in a while. Mama Jaguar. She was a wonderful lady who treated me like a daughter, we laughed we cried we prayed and most of all we had a Godly love that even though she has passed away, the love of God we have for each other, has never left. She was so excited about my faith which is COGIC, there is nothing like the Church of God in Christ. She told me that she had a friend that was Cogic whose name is Mildred Spriggins. She called her and we all spoke and got acquainted another happy moment among the daffodils. Each Sunday after church, Reggie and I would leave church at Macedonia Church of God in Christ and go and visit Mama Jaguar. Church life is my foundation though, I soon met Missionary Alma and Elder William Bolden and it was a blessing to serve them. They enjoyed my cooking, and I enjoyed their company. God is using me for His Glory and my good. He has given me many assignments especially in the Church of God in Christ. I remember meeting Mother Millhouse and Missionary Patricia Wideman, who gave me my first assignment while attending the Holy Convocation in Memphis Tennessee. A church Missionary who was teaching the class had stomach flu and decided that she was going back to the hotel. She asked if I would teach the class and with the approval of Mother Millhouse, I did. We were able to get class underway. I taught the class, and we raised the offertory, prayed, and dismissed the class. It was a blessing from God. I called Missionary Millhouse in hopes that she would be teaching the next session and she did. Praise God. Well after a week of Praise and Worship, large blinging hats, suits, and shimmery attire all over the place, lots of prayer requests, praise reports it was time to return home, back to work I go. Oh yeah did I tell you that I was I got a better paying job? Know you know. I came to work for Guaranty Corporation in 1998. I was working temporarily for a law firm called, Adams and Reese as a receptionist of course. There was a secretary whose name was Barbara Cutrer, who informed me that Guaranty Income Life Insurance company was looking for a receptionist. She referred me to her husband who was the boss there, and asked would I consider applying? I said yes, I met her husband and he made me an offer and I remember when I came for the interview, the receptionist was asleep. The phone rang and woke her up. That answered my question why they were replacing the receptionist. She was delusional when the phone rang, she said "HELLO" sounding as if she was hiding from the police. She called downstairs, I was greeted by

Helpful Holy Hints

Georgia Harris who escorted me to Butch Cutrer, the hiring manager. He was a short stocky fellow with a big howdy-doody smile. I worked with him for over 10 years, some good times and a very few bad. He loved to shop and could make a food spread. Overall, he was a good man, and I am still here now and even though he passed away, Georgia retired, and many changes have taken place I remain thankful for him hiring me. When I first came to Guaranty, I remember my first day was very busy and there was a representative from Eatel whose name was Jenny Parker, she passed away with cancer in later years. She had a list of employees and 15 minutes for me to learn because she had another appointment and time was of the essence, quoting her. She left in 10 minutes and I was out here on my own to learn names, departments, and everything essential to keep this job. There was one thing I noticed when people would come in the lobby, they would often walk by and I would belt out a loud HEY! Often it would scare them out of their whit's, however it was my only means of breaking the ice and allowing them to introduce themselves. I remember one of my favorite people in the entire organization, George Andrew Foster, Jr. He was the boss, the owner. He walked in the front door and said Good morning with a smile, and I said Good morning and I introduced myself and asked him could he get me this job on a permanent basis, knowing that I was already hired. He did not know if I was a temporary or a regular employee. He politely said he would see what he could do. Well, this was asked to everyone who entered the lobby until everyone found out that I was like the little boy who cried "Wolf". Mr. Foster was someone who had so much heart and a very kind and humble demeanor. I remember one day he was riding in the car with colleagues, he called into the office and I answered the phone It's a Great Day at Guaranty Group, good morning. He responded, Hi Judy Martin-Davis I responded what do you want Jr.? Everyone in the car was laughing so hard and I knew I was fired! He comes into the office later that evening and I was just mortified. As a matter of fact, it was the most embarrassing moment of my entire time ever. I quickly walked over and apologized for the earlier call and asked him did he feel disrespected? He said no and he told me he would have felt disrespected if I called him Mr. Foster. No one in the organization would dare call him anything less than Mr. Foster; I am the tyrant in the Guaranty family always getting into trouble. The years I worked with Mr. George A. Foster aka "JR was never a dull moment, we laughed, and we had a ritual, when he would come in, I always have a Kleenex which was known between

Helpful Holy Hints

just us two as a sniffer for him to wipe his nose. Mr. Foster loved lemon ice-box pie from the local Piccadilly, and I would get him one for birthday, Father's Day and occasionally for Christmas. He died the early morning of April 18, 2018. I attended the visitation at Rabenhorst Funeral home and the funeral services took place at Broadmoor Baptist Church. His son, Flynn Foster, did the tribute on behalf of the family giving the History, Life, and Legacy of his father, what a journey, what a guy. We took the rest of the day off and that was truly a blessing. I have served as receptionist faithfully at Guaranty for almost twenty-three years. The journey overall has been wonderful. I meet so many people from all walks of life, from the homeless to the want to be high and trying to be mighty, I welcome them all. Guaranty Income Life insurance company was sold. They moved out to another Baton Rouge location. The insurance company has branched off to another name- Kuvare Holdings. I met the group of 1 lady and several gentlemen, Carlos, Dherron, Steven, David, and Laura. All of them were very cordial. Carlos was very impressed with my large lens sunshades that are called stunners. He tried on a pair and we took a picture just another memorable time at Guaranty with Kuvare. We are Guaranty Corporation and Guaranty Media. There are several radio stations from talk radio to classic rock. Guaranty is so community oriented and very supportive of Southern University, the Gala on the Bluff along with the continuing support of the SU Media Scholarships has continued without missing a beat. Another wonderful chapter of Guaranty is the outreach to Cristo Rey Franciscan High School students- we are several years in and these students have been wonderful. Patricio Castillo has been with Guaranty for 4 years graduated as Valedictorian of his 2021 class, and Marcus Coates is graduating next year. I am so proud of both of them. The journey has been great watching them grow. These students are high goal setting achievers with so much heart and a passion to succeed. That's the upside but there has also been a period of loss for me. Lots of losses that is sometimes hard to put into words. As I struggle through the daffodils of loss, it takes me to a place of remembrance and as each memory fade into the sunset. I laugh, I cry and forever love the moment that has been cemented in time; I had to take a moment and remember the persons who have brought me to the place in life that I am, especially in the ministry. The talks that were often talks of chastisement were the permanent foundations that secured a life of integrity for me. I remain grateful for that. Time has swept these people into the Arms of Jesus and in the bosom of Abraham like the old folks would say. However, these principles kept me grounded and rooted in the faith of our Lord and Savior Jesus Christ. Lord, I thank you for the gift of these lives that have changed my life forever for the good. I am encouraged. I remember these people forever.

Jessie Lee Thomas Flakes Martin- My mother, my Rock. I will always remember all the great moments we had together; you sacrificed your happiness for mine. You worked while I played and had the best childhood a mom could give all by yourself. Mom I cry daily for you. You are loved, missed, and so needed. Now that I am older and wiser, all I have is the memory of your smile and the teachings that will always remain. Thank you for life and most of all thank you for love. Thank God for you. Jessie Martin, "The True Queen, I remember you for life.

Gertrude and Bobby Walton-Gertrude you were the world to me. I learned all my prim, proper and prissy ways from you. Thanks for always paying my rent and for extra money for clothes and beauty. I hated how you treated mom, but for all the love and extras you gave to me, even when I was not so nice, thanks for acceptance and thank and love God for you.

Stuart Paul Wilkerson- my son. 5 short years but a lifetime of your love, I miss you so much, however the one thing I thank God for is that I was blessed to be the chosen mom for your care. You will always be special and etched deep in my heart. I often wish you were right here, gone too soon, but never forgotten. I love and remember you. Jesus is Lord!

Marie Williams- You washed, combed, and brushed my tangled hair when mom did not know how. You fed and kept me for free. Thank God for you.

Mr. and Mrs. Starring, you shared your food and home with me when mom was working. Thank God for you.

Mrs. Alice Wilson-You were my 4th grade teacher who went that extra mile to make sure I was fed, clothed, and taught how to have respect and dignity-Thank God for you.

Mrs. Edna Lucy-my pre-kindergarten teacher who changed my dirty diapers and always made sure that I was safe and had a warm bed, bath, and something to eat while mom was working nights. I love you, thank you.

Helpful Holy Hints

Mrs. Edna Mitchell- You took me as your own. Darryl who has passed on, Cheryl, and Dwayne who remain, you are so blessed to have had Ms. Mitchell as a mom, me too. For all the dinners and teenage years, you frowned, fussed and loved at the same time. I thank God for you.

T.J and Mozelle Edwards-I thank God for the blessing of these 2 people. Thanks for loving and making me part of your family for the cost of nothing. I thank you. I thank God that when you gave me away in marriage the first time, your tears and kind eyes got me through every moment of the wedding. T.J and Mozelle Edwards I remember you. You never hesitated to sit me down and talk to me only like a dad and mom would talk to their daughter. I thank God for both of you. You have left this life but never my heart. I love you both and thank God for both of you.

Carly McCord- She was one of my angels, just gone too soon. Often, I want to go in Tiger studio, but your memories are so strong when we would say GUH BYE. I cannot bear the thought having lost you. We made the cutest video and when I look at it, need I say more?

Doris Hardnett- I remember when I finally had the chance to meet you for the very first time right next door to my office at Mount Zion Baptist Church. Doris was a PE Teacher at McKinley High School for 44 years. She was so proud that for the first time we met and immediately acknowledged each other as cousins. I visited her home often; she encouraged me always be the best that I can be. She passed away, but for the short years we laughed and loved God first and our families, I thank God for you.

Mr. John Cutrer. John was the maintenance man for Guaranty Media who would do anything to help. If I needed something hauled in his truck, he would do it. Sickness hit his earthly body, he moved to a house not made by man's hands. He lived well and finished strong. Thanks for loving me and my family. We loved you in life and in death we cherish you oh so dear. Thank God for you and all those wonderful memorable moments. I remember and cherish and love you tirelessly for life.

Mrs. Marian Patterson- Marian coordinated both of my weddings. I got married at the tender age of 17 and Marian's first thought was to sit me down and have that motherly talk that I already had with my mom. My dad refused to participate because he thought that I was too young and since I was not pregnant, he felt that I was chasing a fantasy, he was right. Nonetheless, Marian dragged me off to Dr. Cummings in South Baton Rouge and I was not pregnant. We proceeded to plan this huge wedding and that it was, with the popular colors pink and pearl white. Marian was one among many mothers for me, she only wanted what was best, especially on my wedding day. She refused money and I was the most beautiful bride in the world to her and mom. Her daughter Carolyn Williams is my inspiration texting me daily to keep me encouraged and empowered. Marian left a ram in the bush her daughter Carolyn to daily inspire and encourage me on this journey called Life.

Betty Isom- The Creole Queen of Fashion. You dressed me like a queen. I remember her catering both of my weddings. The food was amazing how she cooked and made me the happiest woman in world. She showed me how to dress like a lady and live the lifestyle that the Lord who is the Master Weaver of life wanted me to live. Betty had twin sons Michael and Malcolm, along with a daughter Kim. We all grew up together and caught the school bus together. All of them teased me because I was the only one whose mom would be waiting with me at the school bus and all the other moms would walk their children there and leave them. My mom waited until the bus came and would have that 5 minute chat, kept all of us in line at the same time and I was teased all the way to school about it in addition to the way my voice sounded, which I annoys me to this day. Betty played a very exciting role in my life especially when she retired from the state after 30 plus years of service. She had an awesome boutique of hats, suits and specialized in eel-skin purses that was styling and profiling at its finest in those days. I remember her gentle spirit. She adopted me as her own and loved me as a daughter. One of her other loyal customers, first lady Mary Gordon who lived in New Orleans and was one of my dearest friends was so near and dear to my heart. They are together with our other crew. First lady Lands of California, Betty, Mary Gordon, and I was in the dressing crew of four. They all left me here to continue working out my soul salvation.

Charles Nelson Scott-my friend who was also an only child, just like me. He was very shy. He loved to fish, hunt, the outdoor life was his kingdom. He was a bricklayer then an Allstate Insurance agent/owner until his health failed and he soon passed away. He taught me one thing about life insurance and that was to use it exclusively to bury yourself and family, nothing else. Yes sir!

Rev Isadore Primus- the man who loved life and people, you were a gift of teaching and you reminded me that I could do anything but fail if I stay in the will of God.

Bob Bishop- I remember when I first decided to write this book when my son was the tender age of 16 and I told you the fear I had when the first publisher died then the second one died, they were husband and wife if that helps any, and you Bob said do not quit, write the book. I did. Gone too soon. Again, please bear in mind that these publishers were husband and wife and loved it each other so much, the thought of being without each other is what killed him after she died.

I remember you Gladys Ambrose, you gave me the gift of song. I once had the voice of an angel; I kept this gift that God and you gave me under a bushel of silence and never used this gift for your glory dear Lord. Today I regret not utilizing this great gift that would please You. However, I sing the song, Use me Lord with my best voice daily for your glory. I remember this great woman of God who loved to play piano and sing the songs of praise and she skillfully tried teaching me piano lessons as well and I never wanted to learn them. I regret the rejection that I gave and I saw the sadness in her eyes. The lessons were free, and she strived to teach me and I was not willing to learn. But thank God for women like Gladys Ambrose who paved the way adding to me life the fine gift of integrity. Gladys Ambrose, I remember you.

Missionary Dorothy Mae Irving Nelson- I remember you, great woman of God. You nourished my spirit with laughter and taught me the attributes of fashion and finesse, you dressed me from head to toe in the finest clothes that money could buy. You reminded me with each encounter that I was fearfully and wonderfully made. As a first lady you reminded me that I too was one of God's finest creations and never accept anything less than God's best. Missionary Dorothy Mae Irving Nelson, I will always remember you.

Cathleen Henderson- You were the church pianist who took me as your own, fed me brought me to church then to your home and more than anything I remember you singing the song Count on me as the church choir marched in. The one thing I will always remember of you is that you gave me the love and assurance of a mother that you would do your very best to keep me safe and shielded from the evil of this world. Those boxed cakes with butter and occasional homemade icing I will never forget. Thanks for loving me and my mom. Cathleen Henderson, you made a difference in our church and you taught me godliness to keep the faith, and the faith will keep you. Cathleen Henderson, I remember you.

Sheila Hilton- oh Lord my shield, you are the Glory and the lifter of my head. Sheila Faye Hilton my mama sister and very best friend departed this life January 1, 2018 my year was hit by a wrecking ball, day 1. I mentioned her earlier in this project, however she comes to mind so strongly. This is a Sheila Hilton missing my sister I never had- moment. We laughed, we cried, we played dress up like sisters do and I feel such a void in my life without her. I remember the Saturday visits at her dress shop, we were a HOT MESS! She was so dainty and soft spoken, never harsh, or angry, Just SWEET! I cry for your loss; however, I remain faithful to God that even though His Will has been accomplished that He makes no mistakes! He Reigns, HE IS GOOD, and HE IS GOD! Besides, Him there is none other. I thank you Lord God for this kind soul who is gone from this life who now resides with you Lord. I do not understand how cancer took her so fast, but I know that she loved me enough to text me the last day she was alive a picture of the 2 of us and another gentleman who I just don't remember. She loved my cooking, her favorite was lima beans, collard greens, bacon bottom cornbread, my Sunday pot roast. I think she loved anything I cooked, and she would be sprawled out on the couch sound asleep before I could walk out of the room. I would leave her watching television and before long the television would be watching her. She often wanted me to enter any type of food cook off and she would often try to convince me that I would win. She left before I could enter that cook off and write this book, which is something I deeply regret. However, one thing I have learned as I journey through the field of daffodils, the journey is long and hard, however, there are opportunities upon opportunities to accomplish great things which I have done that through the guidance and grace of God. She gave me so many wise talks to make me remember that there is nothing great that I will accomplish in my own strength, but only through God's help. In this stage of my life, I need the strength of God to get through the upcoming holidays without her and my mom, who are in the Arms of Jesus. Shelia Faye Hilton, tearfully I remember you.

Helpful Holy Hints

Rev and Mrs. Isaac and Gertie Ponds- I remember you both taking me to the store to get ice-cream and one day there was a huge roach at the bottom of my cup because I didn't wash the cup and you reminded me that cleanliness is next to Godliness, wash that cup before putting the ice-cream in it. I suggested you call the exterminator, I got another whipping for being a smartie-pants, from her and then got home and mom matched it. TRUE STORY!

Mr. Eddie Rogers- The last conversation we had, it was a Friday you had just visited your cardiologist and he told you that you were healthy as a horse. Over the weekend while cutting grass, you passed away and broke our hearts here at Guaranty. You were a gentle giant with lots of laughs and heart of love for everyone here at work. You were amazing, I miss you hiding behind the door in our old sales department and saying BOO as loud as you could to spook me, oh yeah you scared the snot out of me, only 10 years together, but your kindness will rest in my mind a lifetime. Eddie Rogers. I remember you.

Carol Ashley- I remember the mother daughter bond that we had that even the separation by death can never destroy. I remember when I first came to Guaranty you took me on a journey that enhanced and empowered the mission department of my ministry. You introduced me to a mission organization called Wycliffe. We went to several banquets and fellowships as a family. I remember the last time I visited you at the Baton Rouge General hospital and you told me and our ministerial team that you were tired of fighting the hardships your illness. You said would be in heaven cheering for me as I answer the telephone at work. You also promised that when you make it to heaven you would remind the Lord of my passion for his people and you will wait for me in heaven. I thank God for the moments of talks, laughs, and love that you shared with me and my ministry. You taught me how to be patient and wait on the Lord. For they that wait on the Lord shall renew their strength, they shall mount up on wings like an eagle, run and not be weary, they shall walk and not faint. I am encouraged as I love and remember you, Carol Ashley.

Dr. Stella Righteous- The woman preacher with so much fire and flare. I remember your passion for people getting saved. Dr. Righteous often reminded me when keeping me in prayer that I must take Spiritual Risks to make my journey not easier, yet more defined and refined in the Spirit Realm. These are the tools she gave me, and I am using them daily. 2 Timothy 1:7- God has not given us a spirit of fear, but of power and love and a sound mind along with 2 Corinthians 10:4. For the weapons of our warfare are not carnal, but mighty through God to the pulling down of strong holds;). There have been countless numbers of losses that have almost made me check myself into an asylum, but not just yet. I reflect on how the good days somehow outweigh my bad days; I will not complain. I have so much to be thankful for. There were times during these losses, only a few I have named in this book that I wanted to quit, just runaway. But no way. I have got so much kingdom building to do. There are people out there who are counting on me to complete the work of Him that has sent me by day, because the night is coming where no man or in my case no woman can work. How many times do we get caught up in the madness and rat race of our feelings and miss the great manifestation that God has in place for us? We cannot lose focus on our Father who is the author and finisher of our faith. We will experience, job loss, health issues, loss of loved ones, we will sometimes face financial upheaval and strife. BUT GOD is able to do exceedingly and abundantly in whatever we ask or hope for, but it must line up with the Will of God. We are encouraged with His Word, His Will, and His wonderful way. Sometimes we look at the glass as being half empty, instead of the glass being half full. I am not going to be ungrateful, because God has been so good and no matter what we go through, He is able to keep us from falling even during our challenges and vicissitudes. He is God. I am so caught up in the results of His Will, the finished product, until I often wonder what's next. I remember back in 1991, Stuart had just passed away and we went to the Crawfish festival and had a wonderful time. Soon after we were headed home and out of nowhere, we were hit by a drunk driver whose license were expired, rejected inspection sticker, no auto insurance, and the police officer who the other driver called was her boyfriend and he gave me a ticket. I cannot believe this was happening but oh Lord it was. BUT GOD! My house we were renting was in the newspaper for sale, my husband was laid off his job, it was a rough time, BUT GOD! I received the check from the insurance company that was mistakenly made payable to Bank ONE! What? Not good, the 1990 Ford tempo was paid for so why the check would be made out to the both of us? I called Bank 1 and the rude receptionist answered the telephone and the Holy Spirit reminded me that her mistake would turn my situation into a breakthrough. I was coming out of all of this. I was so upset by all of this and her answering the telephone so rudely made me ask for the Vice-President of the branch, whose

Helpful Holy Hints

name is Janie Spann. I explained my situation to her, and she asked me if I would bring in my check and she would take care of it. She said the same thing to me that the Holy Spirit reminded of and that was I WAS COMING OUT! I could not see the forest for the trees. I was so angry and confused about the whole situation, so perplexed and my soul was vexed. Suddenly when I made it to the Sherwood Forest branch, I met Janie Spann who was a life saver. She asked me if the house had been sold, I said to the best of my knowledge, no. She asked for John Halley's the owner's telephone number and when she called him and asked whether the property had been sold, he said no and immediately asked if she wanted to buy it? She said yes. He faxed over the purchase agreement and she asked if I would be available to meet at Lawyer's Title to close the deal on the house at noon the next day. I said yes. She also told me to let the errand runner drop me off at Coleman Oldsmobile right on the money right on the price was the slogan, unfortunately no longer are Oldsmobile's around. I purchased a 1993 Oldsmobile Cutlass Sierra, burgundy and fully loaded. Things were really getting so much better, the house closed the next day as planned, new car and my husband went back to work. Oh, what a Mighty God we serve. I started working temporarily at Exxon Chemical. Look at God. He moved again as he always does. Janie Spann never took a credit application, she typed up the paperwork combined both house and car with one note of 434.10 and put the payment out 6 months. She also told me if we couldn't pay then no worries, she would delay payment until we were able to pay. This car remained until July 2016 when the motor blew out on the Bonnet Carre' Spillway, near New Orleans, LA. James was coming back from Essence festival 2014. This car was replaced with a fully loaded Chevy Impala. This is just one of many testimonies that God has given nothing shy of miracles. I am so blessed that amid every situation and circumstance that God has delivered me and has never failed. I am a believer that there are three things that God cannot do, He cannot lie, change or fail. In 2010 God gave me a vision to start the show Jags for Jesus for 30 minutes on Thursday and Sundays at 7p.m., we often listen to the Word of God by Bishop Edward Higginbotham then we open the floor for comments. Earl White gives us highlights on all the action that is taking place at Southern University. We close with a prayer and end the call. In 2014 God allowed me to meet an insurance agent Donna Harris who called Guaranty, we talked, and she introduced me to the Morning Watch Prayer line. I called in and people from across the world would chime in and would

Helpful Holy Hints

give prayer requests, praise reports and different topics of interest would come up. We then get into the Word of God, someone will lead us in a song, and someone will close us out in prayer. The facilitator will close us with her Godly remarks of encouragement and empowerment then we would end the call. I thank God that for the first time August of 2015 Apostle Pam Kelly introduced me to the 21-day Daniel Fast, many signs and wonders developed from the fast along with weight loss goals as well. I thank God that this prayer line is in conjunction with God's Word. I am encouraged and so blessed by this daily Movement of God that has ushered me into a new way of worship and giving God His first fruits of praise and worship. I often thank God for people like Pastor Carnell Bailey who has passed on, that put the much-needed fire under me to complete this book. They begged, they prayed and pleaded, now I am doing the work, putting all these daffodils in perspective. When I went to Louisville, Kentucky to serve in a homeless shelter it was so humbling, I attended the Morning Watch Prayer line luncheon, and it was a blessing. I stayed at the Hilton Garden Inn. I attended the luncheon at Cracker Barrel that was housed right next door and what a great time. The food was surprisingly good, and the fellowship was phenomenal. I met in person for the first time

Apostle Pam Kelly, Phyllis Brown, Minister Shelia Clark, Minister Joyce and her daughter Tawana, Kelly Covington, and a few other nice ladies. What a blessing. The next day we went to the Lords' kitchen. I had a chance to serve the homeless, listen to their stories and thank God each day, that it did not happen to me or my family. This is my bucket list to serve in homeless shelters in all 50 states. The Lord's kitchen was homeless shelter number 17. Leaving Louisville, I left my Apple tablet in the airport and some wonderful person turned it in. I was able to get it back within 2 weeks with postage of only 30.00, another miracle, Look at God. Won't He DO IT! Yes, He will. I have passion for many things because life has so much to offer. Let's talk about passion my first passion of course is for God who is my source and Giver of every good and perfect gift. My second passion aside from family is the homeless. I have been blessed to have a homeless family that for hours I bring food, drinks and snacks and we sit under the bridge downtown talk about their goals, encounters and then prayer and is offered. Sometimes we find ourselves working up a Holy Ghost lather, just a movement that has such a profound impact on my life as well as theirs. Ministry is my life, it's my world because God is the depth of my very being-real talk. Here is another gift he has blessed me with the gift to

Helpful Holy Hints

serve as the babysitter of Southern University. I thank God for this school each day of my life. In 2004 spending time with Mama Jag each Sunday, she told me about the need for spiritual enhancement and love for Southern. She reminded me that when she was gone that she would need someone to love that school as she did, unconditionally. She was amazing, she wanted to name me Mama Jaguar, however I learned that no one can ever take a mother's place when she has departed this life, they can only occupy the space and that is what I am doing and will do for life. I was given the name by Mr. Willard Louis Labrie, an old friend who was sitting at the Kappa house at Southern University talking about the destiny of this expensive hobby and he came up with Lady Jaguar. I then shared the name with mama Jag, and she agreed. She instructed me to run out on the side-lines and see what happens. I did in 2003 start working this out, and now it is 2021 and I'm officially called Lady Jag with the non-profit copy right LLC and all. I am godly proud to know that there are many people out there that are excited, and they often share my vision in my efforts to do all the good I can, while I can, with what I can, if I can. Sometimes in my effort to do great things I am often stifled with negative people who will test my kindness and take my meekness for weakness. Two years ago the first of the year

2016, the Lord gave wise counsel to the tables of my heart and reminded me that in-spite of all the great things that He has allowed me to accomplish that He would allow me to do even greater things with His help. John 14:12. What a test it was when there was a shooting here in Baton Rouge and I was contacted by a family member who asked for assistance and when offering to do the family repast following the funeral services, I asked how many people we were preparing for and I was told 5,000 people, I almost fainted. I literally dropped the phone. God forewarned and forearmed me that even greater things would be accomplished, however I never expected this task to manifest this quickly, 8 months later. That period of time sounded like a long time, but this was a first time to be given such a huge task, however when you believe the Bible from Genesis to Revelations, it instructs you in Philippians 4:13 that you can do all things through Christ that strengthens you. But often you may know the Word, believe the bible, but when it is time to put your faith and belief in action, it is sometimes very difficult. Therefore, it is so important that you daily equip yourself with the Word of God, Ephesians 6:11, you do it by putting on the whole armor of God, so you will be able to fight the wickedness and darkness of this world. We must have sound doctrine daily to be able to face our

Helpful Holy Hints

daily challenges and walk in Victory. I thank God daily, all day every day for His Favor that He has placed upon me with all the Saints of God that remind me of my declaration through Christ Jesus. For example, Brother Perry Musgrow another one of my brothers, and brother J.J. Jobe one of our radio artist, reminds me daily via text what my declaration for Victory is, and how I will be victorious in the things of God. He pin-points that even during the storms, that's when breakthrough is just around the corner. I am convinced that when life is blowing its strongest winds, that's when God is about to bring you out into a destiny of overflow. That is real talk people. I know that sometimes the stems on your daffodils are thin and an eyesore for your faith to work through. You often encounter negative and spiritually dead people who have given up on the faith and have no faith fight left. There are so many people who are walking around spiritually dead and diminished in the things of God. There is no reason in the world to give up on God because in-spite of all the times we are often useless, unfaithful and in our fleshly ways, He understands and is often standing there with wide open arms ready and willing to accept us just as we are. Despite it all, He accepts us with all our baggage, selfish ways, and issues. Yet He died for all of us. He never changes; He remains a God of order, kindness, and love. Reminding us that with all we are dealing with, He is right there with us. He promised never to leave nor forsaken us. We leave and abandon Him daily when He tells us to go right, we go left. He tells us to not be conformed to this world but be ye transformed through the renewing of your mind. We do it our way all day every day and when we get to the end of our rope and we mess up we want to call on Jesus, and that is ok He stands so tall and patient. Often when things are well with us, He is the last person we include. He desires to share in our joy as well as our sorrow. He is God and beside Him there is no other. He wants us to be encouraged and saturated with His Word so when the enemy attacks us we do not run, we fight back with THE WORD! He reminds us in Isaiah 59:19 "So shall they fear the name of the LORD from the west, and His glory from the rising of the sun. When the enemy shall come in like a flood, the Spirit of the LORD shall lift up a standard against him." Talking to so many people I have very few people that I call friend. I want to make mention that when my best friend Sheila Hilton passed away in 2017, I met a very similar friend whose name is Denise Lockett. My bestie, and her mom the lovely Mrs. Mercedes Livingston who she shares with me and her Dad, met him once who had me laughing for days while fussing with Denise, talking trash big time. My gorgeous niece Jasmine aka Jazzy Raye, Denise's daughter has labored in prayer with me through many disappointments from world hurt to church hurt, they care, they share, they love and cherish our relationship in their own unique way. I love it. It is all God. Denise reminded me that the work of God must continue, and I thank God that today we share so much in common. We are both only children and we often talk about our encounters both good and bad and how depending on God always brings us to a place of refuge and freedom in the Spirit. I can count my friends on 1 hand and have fingers left. We are talking real relationships here. I was at a Cogic worker's meeting in Walker, LA maybe 20 years ago. I saw this beauty, Kathleen Harrison. This lady looked so much like my biological mother and her energy is just through the roof. Somehow, we made a God driven connect. We laughed, we talked and spent so much time in the Presence of God. It is never a dull moment when we talk on the phone or just come over and visit, just Jesus. We have often sat for hours laughing and being our royal selves so to speak. But the one thing I love most is that she genuinely loves me like a daughter. Her daughter Claude Range is so sweet and loving, she has such kind eyes, and that soft understanding voice of love and kindness is priceless. Her dog MOO SHOO, also known as the broke down Plank Road Pimp, with his back side sitting on a heating pad for real. He is the man of the house and rules well. I remember when we first met, she had an old black cat whose name was "Spooky". He was so affectionate; he would rub his body against my legs and would not stop until you acknowledge his presence. He passed away and that was a sad moment in the daffodils. On a happier note. I would like to highlight in these series of books to come, how God has blessed me with people I work with Monday through Friday and how these people impact my working environment. Gordy Rush Vice President and General Manager of Radio. I have been soliciting Santa for just a small neck for him to enhance his breathing. I have worked with Gordy for almost 23 years he makes my day. Even though I tease him about his neck, he still loves me and calls me momma just like most of the team. I remember when Flynn came to work at Guaranty, no one could have told me that he would not be that bougie micromanaging boss that would give employee's a hard time. But He treat all of us with respect and dignity that all employees so rightfully deserve. Flynn has a special passion for Chicken Shack chicken and dirty rice. Maybe when I get ready for that pay raise, I will bring him a that chicken and dirty rice

Helpful Holy Hints

and see what happens. I remember when I first came to Guaranty his wife Dana would bring their 2 boys Luke and Landon and they were the cutest kids and now they are all grown up, gone to college and they are taller than Flynn. T.J. Solis, the father to Princess Kennedy and his lovely wife Hillary got to include Prince Jewels their pup who has been so supportive of my many events, thank you for loving me and when the Saints go marching in, I know you all will be in that number. I surely plan to. Forrest Mills, Chief Financial Officer who came to the organization around the same time I did, I thank God for your heart that cares and not to mention his son Steven Mills who is another one of my sons. God has answered many prayers of mine on his behalf and the best is yet to come for the entire Mills family in Jesus Name. I recently met a young man whose name is Alexander Adams of Crimer. He rents office space, and I can remember I was going home to cook for the homeless and he ordered tons of barbecue for his team and there was so much food left over and he gave it all to me to feed the homeless, what a blessing. He is on his way to doing great things is what I speak into his life. He also gave Crimer shirt makes me feel like an honorary part of Team Crimer. I must make mention of Darlene Cooper who I have worked with for 23 years. Darlene has such a cute way of approaching me, she will gently say Good morning, what's going on? If I am wearing a new outfit she will ask, "Is that new? Just sweet. I have also had the honor of working with Cindy Ussery for 23 years and she has been a God send to me. I often ask her some of the most ridiculous wellness and payroll questions and she is accurate down to the penny. Thank you, Cindy, for all those times when I needed change for a 20, along with other craziness you are always looking out for me. YOU ROCK! James and daughter Madison Gilmore, what a sweet pair. James bridged a gap about 5 years ago. I had an old video tape that was the words of my late son Stuart who told me that I should make a video of him comforting me in his final days, I agreed. As time went on my VCR broke, we trashed it and I was sitting at my desk and James walks in and asks what was wrong I told him that I had been holding on to this video tape and what I wouldn't give to have it remastered so I could see and listen to it. James with that Santa Claus smile said I can do that it is nothing to do. He made 5 DVDS the very next day and I almost fainted. James Gilmore is truly Santa, all year long. I admire is willingness to help others no matter what. His daughter Madison came to work at Guaranty, and she was the rug rat of the station, and she would come in and have our daily chat and off to work she would go, I

Helpful Holy Hints

miss her working her, but I must cut the apron strings and her fulfill her dream and that's to work at Disney World in Orlando Florida where she is right now. She must now go and grow. Which brings me to my other son Matt Moscona. I am so prayerful and thankful for all the times he calls me mama. He and his wife Erica what a lovely couple, and let us not forget their son drummer Drew. A few times Matt and Drew have chimed into my Jags for Jesus Show and we could hear Drew just drumming away, how sweet. Matt gave me my first Yeti cup and often reminds me especially when I am fasting "NO BREAD"! He also tells me that I better not harass anyone when they come into the lobby! Do I listen? Go Figure! He has lost a ton of weight; however, he is still addicted to my sweet potato pie. Brittany Rose and Abby Leigh, that is the Blonde Tour age. These ladies have taken off like a rocket with off the Record with Brittany and Abby. I am so proud of them. Rick Cantu my Savior on the job. He goes to Costco's picks up breakfast, it gets no better thank Rick. I remember he went to Costco's on his lunch break, and I gave him my check book and driver's license. Rick was horrified to tell me he lost my driver's license. I guess he thought that I was going to come out of a box on him. But no, I went to Port Allen, sat 3 hours and was all set. I am teasing Rick to this day about that license.

There are so many times when life throws us a curve balls, we are so discouraged that we cannot pray. We are lost for words and often the wounds in our soul are so deep and our problems have put us in a place of depression and has taken all we have left to fight back. There is a familiar passage of scripture that has remained with me down through the ages and it has given me so much encouragement during the losses of so many people that I love. Proverbs 3:5-6 which reads, trust in the Lord with all thine heart and lean not to thine own understanding, but in all our ways acknowledge Him and He will direct our pathway. We must trust when the going gets tough, the tough get going. But we much also realize that sometimes He allows us to go through these tough times not because we have done anything wrong, but because sometimes He is priming, pruning and perfecting us to get us ready for greater things. He is toughening our skin for tough times. I remember a song writer Marvin Sapp, who often say that there are some of us who are desiring some people and some things that we are not ready to take on. He gave a great example that if we were given a Rolls Royce would we be able to maintain it in our present financial situation? Would it be a blessing, or would it be a burden? Would we be able to pay the cost of insurance? If it broke down, would we be able to pay and have

Helpful Holy Hints

it repaired? Sometimes we bite off more than we can chew and when the bottom falls out, we want advice from God, but why not seek Him before we make these decisions in the first place? Why not consult with Him and make Him inclusive of what we can do, so He can do what He does best and that is lead and guide us in the way that we should go. He is often left out of our initial plans, and when the going gets tough and we cannot figure out what we need to do, we go running to Him with all these excuses of why we did what we did. But, if we would have consulted with Him first and trusted His decision which may have been tight but right, we would not be in this predicament in the first place. But when the bottom falls out and the people whose ideas, we trusted in the first place left you hanging, would not take your calls, had every excuse under the sun why they cannot help you and there stands God. Have you ever trusted someone and found a safe place of comfort in their character and come to find out that they were lying, stunting, and fronting, bucking and bogarting about who they are? Have you ever thought you could count on someone and when the rubber met the road, they were all talk and no action and when you needed them most, they failed you? Yes, we all have experienced this dark feeling, that put us in our feelings of loneliness and gloom. But one thing I know that the struggles of this world can leave you in a lonely place and some of the people that you thought would never deceive you, they did. They stole your dreams that you shared with them instead of God. They murdered, annihilated, and sometimes even destroyed your ambitions and used it for their own greed, BUT GOD. Always remember that sometimes by letting people in on your ideas they will blindside you by telling you all the things you want to hear and meaning none of them. They wish you well, pat you on the back and tell you all the right things for all the wrong reasons. Just to give you a heads up, this reminds me of another favorite passage of scripture that is often thought provoking but so true. Romans 8:28 which until a few years ago I learned that there is a part of that passage that never came to mind when reading it. It reads; All things work together for good for those that love the Lord and are THE CALLED ACCORDING TO HIS PURPOSE. I had it reading, all things work together for good for those who are called, not "THE CALLED" like it is written, but just are called according to His purpose. I thank God for people like Apostle Pam Kelly who gave me the ultimate heads up on how this scripture is to be properly interpreted. God is so good, and He is worthy to be praised. Each day I desire and long for more bible knowledge on how to ultimately seek and serve

Him first and then serve His people. I am blessed to have learned the majority of my bible knowledge from Bishop "E.J" Higginbotham, Sr. He transformed what was good and made it better for my good. I am thankful that this man gave me the finishing touches of holiness. I would drive him to church, worker's meetings, and Holy Convocations. I would run errands and learn the beauty of holiness in not only being kind to him, but that was the start of the homeless outreach. He taught me how to be always ready to reach out and spread the Gospel to others. When he lived here in Baton Rouge, we would visit hospitals, nursing homes and attended other community events, like Relay for Life by the American Cancer Society and he would kick off the survivor lap. The Southern University Gala on the Bluff, which is the Southern University Annual Scholarship fundraiser, just to name a few. I am grateful for the uncompromised word that he brings twice weekly on the Jags for Jesus as the foundational father. He brings the listening audience hope that the word of God is truth and never seem to tire out. I can remember when I first met him, and I was a social drinker, and I was attending a Southern University football game and I offered to bring him a plate from the tailgate site and he agreed. When I came over, he brought to my attention that he smelled alcohol, and I was so embarrassed, that was one of the most embarrassing moments of my life. He politely said to me, have you been drinking? I pretended not to hear him and changed the subject and he asked again in a more authoritative manner and I humbly uttered "yes sir. He said you should be ashamed of yourself. You have no reason to consume alcohol if you are a woman of God. Well, he said if you are not ashamed of yourself, I am ashamed of you. He proceeded to pray for me; I was so ashamed that man prayed the desire to drink alcohol ever again out of my mouth. I went home and there was so much Crown Royal in my house, I emptied every bottle, poured it down the drain and from that day on, I never consumed any alcoholic beverages again, including beer. I was instantly delivered from the shackles of alcohol. I thank God that this was a strong hold and God delivered me. Thank you, Jesus. I have had addictions to marijuana, cigarette smoking of 2 and a half packs per day, but God delivered me and for this I remain grateful. Pastor Higginbotham made such a difference in making me a better servant for the Master. The song that comes to mind very often just before prayer each day is Use Me Lord, in thy service, draw me nearer, every day. I am willing, Lord to run all the way. But if I falter, while I am trying, please don't be angry, just let me stay. Lord I'm willing Lord to run on all the way. I am encouraged by those songs of old that keeps me grounded and rooted in the things of God. Sometimes new school gospel just does not seem to cut it when you are amid a storm that has side swiped you out of your comfort zone in Jesus. There are times when your direct connect to Jesus is blocked or clogged by this life's journey. You can't seem to directly connect to Jesus, and you need a soul stirring stick to your ribs kind of song. You need a breakthrough that will drive you right into the presence of God and not stagnate but usher you with the hand holding of the Holy Spirit that seals and comforts us into His Presence. Are you in a daffodil that is draining your spirit or one that dressing you up for the next phase of God's destiny in Christ Jesus? Where are you in your prayer life? Where are you in the give up, grow up and go up goals? What do you look like in the spiritual mirror of life? Will you be wishing and wanting or doing and dwelling? Will you allow God to do a new thing in you? Will you let go and let God be God? God knows what's best for all of us. This recalls another song, Take the Lord along with you everywhere you go. He takes you on another level of goodness and manifestation that will keep you in perfect peace with a mind stayed on Him. It's a mighty movement that makes you motivated in the things of God, it makes those rough places smooth in the Spirit. It cultivates and carries us to what God's plan is for our lives instead of our own agenda. I need God often which keeps me so aware that He is always nearby. I want God to make my next move and not go alone and plan my agenda without Him. I want to move only by His Spirit that will usher me back into the Masterpiece of His Master Plan. He is so perfect in all His ways and know that when He is holding the reigns of your life, you can never go wrong in the things that you are doing. There may be times when you get in the storm of job loss, people loss, mental loss, financial loss, whatever the case may be. He is always forever present with you into the beginning of the journey, the midst of the journey as well as the end of the journey. Though you slay me Lord, yet will I trust you. That is all a part of the journey of life. It changes but God does not. Let Him into your heart and let Him be God. You must remain soul surrendered daily! I would be so out of order not to mention some other great women of God that have impacted my life. Mrs. Latisha Edney, she was a great woman of God who reminded me when I could not seem to erase that smoking addiction. She prayed and told me that when I was serious about quitting, bring the cigarette pack, we would pray and in Jesus Name, that smoking addiction would go away. It did in

Helpful Holy Hints

Jesus Name. Lady Mildred Johnson of Living Faith Christian Center will call and remind me that she misses me and give so much encouragement during this pandemic. Diane Louis is another Spiritual cheerleader who send reminder texts to inspire and empower my spiritual energy. Shirley Lolis, someone who I don't see very often, but when we go to our favorite restaurant called Acme Seafood, we have a blast. Let's weigh in on Covid 19. This pandemic has broken my heart a minimum of 68 times with so many deaths of people I love. I have been doing most activities like doctor visits, virtually via Zoom. After not being able to get nails done since Valentine's day eve of 2019, I got a nail spa treatment and toenails have grown out long I was able to get them polished for Mother's Day 2021. I am excited that I was able to go to Bumble Lane and get that much needed massage by Donald for Mother's Day. Praise God. Due to Covid-19, me and my family was able to get fully vaccinated for free. We took the Moderna vaccine, I had very little side effects, only tiredness and headaches. I was sharing with my election family when I worked the polls in March of 2021 to make sure the tell Lottie, Dottie, and everybody to get the sleeves up and get vaccinated. What really has made me so aware of how serious this virus is, by seeing so many people lose their lives. We must support this effort and remind people that just because they are vaccinated does not mean they don't need to wear a mask and continue to social distance, wash their hands and spread the word to get vaccinated, so we can stop the spread of this virus. God wants us to be healthy, wealthy, and wise to all the things that will enhance our journey in this life. God desires us to have balance while here on this earth. He wants us to give to the ministry our tithes and offerings so that there will be meat in His house. I thank God for leaders that have a huge heart of tithing and the needs of people. I have always prayed to be connected to a church and leaders that have a heart for the needs of people. I am inspired by people that are concerned about giving a hand up to someone in need which reminds me of Byron and Ethel Comeaux, owners of the Magnolia Care Center Veterans home. Our huge friendship really beefed up when one fine day I needed a ride to New Orleans to pick up credentials for the Southern University Bayou Classic. I asked Byron would he give me a lift since Jeffery Ory was allowing me to pick up my credentials before the game. He told me that he needed to stop at an aunt's house and would only be a moment, but he wanted me to meet her. How cool is this? It is a small world. His aunt, sister Anne Elise of Sisters of the Holy Family on Chef

Helpful Holy Hints

Menteur New Orleans East opened the door and made my day. We laughed and talked about old times when I was in 7th grade, she was one of the angels who made it her business to feed me and my mother. She looked out for clothes and school uniforms and never told a soul that she was the wind beneath our wings there at St. Francis Xavier. It was great seeing her again. Well back to Byron and Ethyl who are so helpful in my many quests. They will help whenever and however they can to make me shine. I can remember one Christmas I had this huge live Nobel fir tree, it was leaning and about to fall. I called Byron, he rushed over and took sticks of wood and all went well. These people genuinely love like the Saints of God are supposed to. I can call them at any time and there they are, always there to help. They are my rocks that make it possible to reach many goals of greatness. I also think about people who make it possible for me to make great strides. Damien Smart, a graduate of Southern University twice. He put my wonderful double monitor computer together and he keeps me connected. One of my favorite students. I can remember when he and his 5 brothers were living next door and they loved to play in my yard, and I would run them out. I have got so many children from many walks of life, but I love them all the same. I must mention another one of my students,

Terrance Cola. I remember when he attended Southern, he was just one of many who received our Guaranty Media Scholarship and he graduated with honors and is presently living in New Orleans, LA. These kids are such an inspiration to my life. They keep me prayerful, especially during the struggle of this pandemic and all the challenges that come with it. I have started back attending church, going to the grocery store, and making some events, like Marcus Coates ring ceremony and Patrcio Castillio's graduation mass and graduation ceremony. I could not miss it for the world. I am fully depending on God to keep the refuge of protection around these young people, this is my sincere prayer as I anchor all my situations and circumstances in His hands. God knows everything about everything. I have struggled in writing this book for His Glory and to help all men women, boys, and girls to keep the faith and remember that the race is not given to the swift or to the strong, but to the one who will hold out to the very end of the ages. Here are more Helpful Holy Hints.

HELPFUL HOLY HINTS

Monday- Remodel your mindset and become a remarkable role-model for the Almighty- Monday!

Tuesday- It's a Must to take the Rust out of your trust-Tuesday

Wednesday-Weight loss at sensible cost makes you healthy wealthy and wise, Wednesday.

Thursday- Take the Victory trolley to triumph over trials and tribulations- Thursday.

Friday- Farewell to the fireworks of fear and frustration. Friday. Fear is only (F)False(E)Evidence(A) Appearing (R) Real.

Saturday-Saints sifting Satan as wheat as we make a solid spiritual foundation and say so long to sorrow- Saturday.

Sunday-Make solid your spiritual foundation and say so long to sorrow Sunday.

More Helpful Holy Hints

Monday-In the midst of the madness, miracles are making their way to a Mighty Manifestation-Monday.

Tuesday-Target the beauty of breakthrough and burst through the bounty of your brokenness with boldness-Tuesday.

Wednesday-Don't' waddle in weakness; rise up in wellness-Wednesday.

Thursday-Tackle tough times of torment and bad temperament with a ticket of Godly opportunities and thankfulness-Thursday.

Friday-The final phase of favor is the fruitfulness of fruition. - Friday.

Saturday- Seeking the Savior is the satisfying solution to sanctification and soul salvation-Saturday.

Sunday-Set the standard in Sanctified servitude that will satisfy the Savior Sunday.

TO INSPIRE AND EMPOWER

Monday-Magnify and get Master motivated for the Master on a magnificent Monday.

Tuesday-Touch-up your testimony with the truth that tough times don't last but tough people take over tough times. Tuesday.

Wednesday-Good Wednesday rest will whisk away your worries with wonderful rewards and wonders of wellness.-Wednesday.

Thursday-Thinking of His Goodness and Godliness helps us to thrive with thankfulness. -Thursday.

Friday-Phase out false hopes and fall into the fantastic favor of the Father. -Friday.

Saturday-Situate your circumstances with a mindset that is innovative, motivated, rejuvenated and consecrated for the Savior.-Saturday.

Sunday-Stop the stinking thinking state of mind and maintain the methods of the Master. Sunday.

HELPFUL HOLY HINTS

Monday-Make the most of the moments in meditation. -Monday.

Tuesday-Tranquilize the tricks of the trader Satan by trusting in triumph-Tuesday.

Wednesday-Wear out the weapons of worldliness with the works of God's wisdom for wellness. Wednesday.

Thursday-Take charge of the challenges with Godly change-Thursday.

Friday-Face your fears with fired up fasting and praying- Friday.

Judy Martin Davis

Saturday-Saints set the standard of saving time being saved, steadfast, and sanctified-Saturday.

Sunday-Saints savoring the Spiritual Salvation of the Savior-Sunday.

Helpful Holy Hints

Helpful holy hints are often such a huge part of my life and sometimes I tend to rely on these hints to better stay focused on the word of God. There is nothing more powerful than the Word of God that properly directs your life to empower and improve your way of thinking and functioning in your journey through the daffodils. There are times of the year when I remember most the things of old. For example, during Resurrection Sunday Season when flowers are budding, and the pollen is in the air I am reminded of the elephant ear flowers and lilies that were my mom's favorites. I would watch her plant them and when they would grow and spread all over the front of the house her face would light up like a child at Christmas time. She was so proud of the spread of these beautiful flowers. My mom was such a beauty. She taught me that the sure way to be blessed was to give with a heart of cheerfulness and thanksgiving and watch the overflow from God. It works Saints. I am so inspired by giving, sometimes it feels even better when you give to someone that you don't know. It blesses me to watch the expression on someone's face, especially the elderly when they get free groceries or just a few dollars for a meal or whatever the need they may have. It blesses my soul to see them smile sometimes it feels like a sigh of relief for them and me too on a spiritual level. Whatever the case may be, I thank you Lord Jesus that the investment that I have made in the betterment of the kingdom, large or small is a destiny push for both, a win win situation. This life will get your mind focused on the things of God when you see the things of this world will disappoint you and send you down many roads that you are not willing to take or able to deal with. The need of every person is a haven in the Lord. Take the time to speak Life to each dark situation and let God led you to the prepared destiny that He has in store for you. In this Christian journey the old Saints used to say, that Salvation is FREE, But it's not cheap. For a very long time I wondered what was meant by that. God loves us and because He has His children on His mind all the time, His thoughts of us brings Him Joy. It pleasured Him to create his people to love and that allowed His Glory to shine through us. He created us in His image and likeness exclusively for His Glory to shine in and through all of us. He wants us to join Him in being the light of the world by saving souls and bringing them to Him. He is determined to utilize our gifts and make them a large part of kingdom building one brick at a time, in this world of uncertainty, disappointment and not to mention disrespect and empty promises. That is the reason why it is so important to stay connected to the word of God on a daily basis in order to

Helpful Holy Hints

keep the things of God in view. It is so important to study the bible and get the word deep down in your soul, to learn life changing lessons. You must study to show thyself approved, as it is so perfectly demonstrated in 2 Timothy 2:15. These are some life changing lessons that I will never forget that I have learned on the Morning Watch Prayer line. There are many lessons that I have learned over time however, I learned a huge little known bible known fact which is; There are 16 verses missing out of the NIV bible and they are as follows: Matthew 17:21, Matthew 18:11, Matthew 23:14, Mark 7:16, Mark 9:44 & 9:46, Mark 11:26, Mark 15:28, Luke 17:36, John 5:3–4, Acts 8:37, Acts 15:34, Acts 24:6–8, Acts 28:29, Romans 16:24, I John 5:7-8. That is one of the main reasons that I have abandoned this version of the bible. I want the entire word, no missing facts, my soul is at stake and I cannot take that kind of spiritual risk. I am a believer who has come to terms with God as well as myself that I want to cover my entire area of understanding in God's sight to not miss my destiny, and that's Heaven. I live for heaven's destiny, and I so deeply desire to maintain a Godly deportment what will satisfy and glory Him in all His Goodness and Faithfulness. The one thing I desire is to give Him TOP-NOTCH PRAISE that He will be pleased with. Not some watered down, no purpose praise that will not please Him or meet His standards. What kind of Worshipper are you? Do you give Him your best praise? Do you worship in how you feel or are you praising your way through your problem amid it all? How do you fight the feeling, when your problems are bigger than your desire to praise Him? Helpful Holy Hints will get you to that mode of Perfect Holiness and prayerfully it will get your mind focused on that simple fact that the Lord will keep your hearts and minds in perfect peace only if you keep your mind stayed on Him. For He is worthy to be always praised people. He is waiting to be offered your first fruits each day. How many times do we waver in the things of God? Take a moment to think about what if you are on the end of your breakthrough and stifle your praise, you may miss the bliss of your breakthrough. Please keep the praise going for His Glory! There are some Helpful Holy Hints that need to be reiterated into your Spirit. Use them to saturate your mind, body, and soul to a point of praise in the Spirit. We must use these spiritual tools to take us to our destiny of greatness. I was listening to the radio and I was heard someone say that there is no such thing as corrective criticism. I laughed, often in the Word of God, Jesus rebuked many to perfect them in the things of God and not in the things of the flesh.

As a seasoned Saint, talking to maybe 20-30 people minimum on a weekly basis, if I see that they are traveling wrong and not using sound judgement and say or do something to start them on the right road to success and greatness in the spirit realm, I have failed God. The Gospel is simply Good News and the good news people is lacking in this time of uncertainty is simple but sound doctrine. Guaranty has implemented a list of fundamental practices that not only can be used to successfully run an organization, but to achieve spiritual goals as well. Here they are: Service always, teamwork, innovation, passionate, integrity, love, and respect, positivity, and fun. Living righteously, be a lifelong learner, and accountability.

Judy Martin Davis

Helpful Holy Hints

To help you through your toughest moments

Monday-Make the most of the moments in meditation. Monday.

Tuesday-Tranquilize the tricks of the trader Satan by trusting in triumph-Tuesday.

Wednesday-Wear out the weapons of worldliness with the works of God's wisdom for wellness. Wednesday.

Thursday-Take charge of the challenges with Godly change-Thursday.

Judy Martin Davis

Friday-Face your fears with fired up fasting and praying- Friday.

Saturday-Saints set the standard of saving time being saved, steadfast, and sanctified- Saturday.

Sunday-Saints savoring the Spiritual Salvation of the Savior-Sunday.

Helpful Holy Hints

Monday-Make your mindset magnificent as you reset your meditation methods. - Monday.

Tuesday-Tally up your testimonies as you target the beauty of your breakthrough. - Tuesday.

Wednesday-Wash your worries away with the wonderful words of Wellness Wednesday.

Thursday-If He brings us to it, He will bring us through it. Thursday.

Friday. Follow in His footsteps and watch His infallible favor fall into fruition. Friday

Saturday-Separating our lives from sin is a soul soothing solution for the Saints. Saturday.

Sunday- Star-studded Saints striving to stay saved. Sunday.

HELPFUL HOLY HINTS

Monday- Make the most of your moments of meditation as you motivate your mindset to magnify the Master-Monday.

Tuesday-Take on the task of thankfulness and thoughtfulness as you take the ti me to teacher others. -Tuesday.

Wednesday-Rebuild and refresh, revive and restore your walls of wellness as you reap the rewards of wisdom. -Wednesday.

Thursday-Heighten your hopes to happier and higher heights, deeper depths and wider widths. -Thursday.

Judy Martin Davis

Friday-Firm up your foundation with a faith fixer-upper and fire up for the favor of the Father. -Friday.

Saturday-Stand up step up and stretch out on the salvation of the Savior. Saturday.

Sunday-Set your mind to celebrate the success of your season-Sunday.

HELPFUL HOLY HINTS

Monday-Modify your mood of madness to a mindset of Meditation-Monday.

Tuesday-Touch up your testimony with the truth that tough times do not last but tough people take over tough times-Tuesday.

Wednesday-Wisk away your worries with wonderful rewards of wellness-Wednesday.

Thursday-Thinking of His goodness and Godliness helps me to thrive with thankfulness-Thursday.

Friday-Phase out false hopes and fall into the fantastic favor of the Father-Friday.

Judy Martin Davis

Saturday-Situate your circumstances with a mindset that is innovative, motivated, rejuvenated and consecrated for Christ.

Sunday-Star-studded Saints striving to stay saved-Sunday.

HELPFUL HOLY HINTS

Monday-Make the most of your moments of motivational meditation as you motivate your mindset to magnify the Master-Monday.

Tuesday- Take the time to talk about Jesus and take on the testimonies to follow-Tuesday.

Wednesday-Rebuild and restore your walls of wellness as you reap the rewards of wonderful Godly wisdom-Wednesday

Thursday- Helpful Holy Hints heighten our hopes to happier and higher heights, deeper depths and wider widths. Thursday.

Friday-Use Friday as your faith fixer-upper as you firm up your foundation and get fired up for the favor of the future-Friday.

Saturday-Stand still and let God shine-Saturday.

Sunday-Set sail for God's show up and show out Sunday.

HELPFUL HOLY HINTS

Monday-Mold and make a memorable masterpiece for the the Master's Master Plan-Monday.

Tuesday-Toot the tunes of God's goodness as you testifiy and let God take total control-Tuesday.

Wednesday-Wipe out the warfare of Wellness with the wonderful willingness to eat well and work out regularly-Wednesday.

Thursday-Take the Praise Him plunge as you Go, Flow, glow and Grow in the things of God-Thursday.

Friday-Firm up your foundation of faithfulness with the full armour of the fruits of the spirit. Friday.

Saturday-Sow your seeds of spirituality into the soil of sanctification-Saturday.

Sunday-Strike out sin as you stay connected to the Savior.-Sunday.

HELPFUL HOLY HINTS

Monday- Make those merry memories as you make a difference- Monday.

Tuesday- Try the Spirit with the Word of thankfulness-Tuesday.

Wednesday-Wait on the Lord and Woosah-Wednesday.

Thursday-Take the time to thank God-Thursday.

Judy Martin Davis

Friday-Put on the full Armour of God and fight the good fight of Faith-Friday.

Saturday-Stand tall in Steadfast word of God Saturday.

Sunday- Say it out loud, The blood still works Sunday.

Helpful Holy Hints

Monday- Make the day go Great for His Glory.- Monday .

Tuesday- Try on the Spirit of trading triumph for trouble. -Tuesday.

Wednesday-Whisk off the weight of worry.-Wednesday.

Thursday-Track your hidden spiritual treasures.-Thursday.

Friday-Find your Favor and fix your mindset to fall in the Favor of God.-Friday.

Saturday-Stay Steadfast and unmovable in the word of God Saturday.

Sunday- Stand steady and stay still as the still small voice shouts Jesus is Lord.-Sunday.

Judy Martin Davis

THE FINAL REMARKS FROM THE AUTHOR.

THE BEST IS YET TO COME!

THE DESTINY, THE FINISH

The destiny for this volume does not end but will pause and take a breather to usher you to your next destiny.
The Dream fields of Volume 2 awaits.
I want to thank those of you who supported me in this project with if nothing more than buying this book as your financial support, thank you. May God bless and keep you always is my sincere prayer.

Judy Martin Davis
Her Eminence, Lady Jaguar-SUBR

The Biography of Judy Martin-Davis

She is Evangelist Judy Martin-Davis affectionately known as Her Eminence Lady Jaguar, Southern University Baton Rouge. She hails from the dirty South of Baton Rouge bottom. Judy attended Baton Rouge High School and was further educated at Commercial and Delta Trade Schools. Her career in Television and Radio took off in 1983, thanks to the late but great Eula Mae Hatter and Mary Mason Gordon. Both women launched into the deep of discipline teaching Judy all she needed to know about radio and moving on to 2 local television stations. Judy has served in media for over 38 years and has currently served 23 of those years with Guaranty Media. The remaining time was with Citywide Broadcasting currently Cumulus Media, and television stations Fox 44 and Channel 33. Judy serves the community in various capacities, heavily involved in ministry, spiritual counseling, and homeless outreach. The name Lady Jag evolved in 2003, after meeting the late great Jewel Jefferson Durr affectionately known as Mama Jag. Since then, she has been dedicated and committed to many outreach activities along with SU Athletics in all sports supporting students with food, financial and spiritual guidance. She reminds them to remember Proverbs 3:5-6 and be reminded that Romans 8:28 are two life changing scriptures. Judy Martin-Davis has deemed her role as a God Given Mission, that allows her to be able to assist at her expense without any financial aid other than the spiritual and financial gifts only provided by our Lord and Savior Jesus Christ. God has ushered her into 2 things, her purpose which is the ministry of Helps and the Favor of God which deems her Blessed and Highly Favored, on Top and Rising to another level of Kingdom building one brick at a time. Judy has a bucket list to complete serving in at least one homeless kitchen in all 50 states and has conquered 19 states so far as of December 2019. To God be the glory. In 2019, Judy wrapped up her 19th mission trip in Atlanta, Georgia serving in the City Rescue Mission. But covid, cruel covid-19 has paused the journey but not

destroyed the destiny. Judy is the Founder of Jags 4 Jesus Ministry which was offered to God in 2010 and has never missed a show. Her daily prayer time begins at 4am to 6:30 a.m. which ushers her into the presence of God daily. Her heart to feel and her hands to harvest blessings for others is her goal.
Great is His Faithfulness to me.

"Keep it Moving Forward in Jesus Name".

Helpful Holy Hints

www.ingramcontent.com/pod-product-compliance
Lightning Source LLC
Chambersburg PA
CBHW071502070526
44578CB00001B/419